ISBN-10: 0-692-87272-8
ISBN-13: 978-0-692-87272-7

Published in the USA

What About Me?

A book by and for an Autism Sibling

By Brennan and Mandy Farmer
Illustrated by Emily Neff

This book is for all of the very special special needs siblings.

My name is Brennan.
I have a brother and a sister.
I love my brother. He is a little
different than me, but that's okay
because it makes him unique.
My brother has autism. His brain
works differently and some things
are harder for him to do.

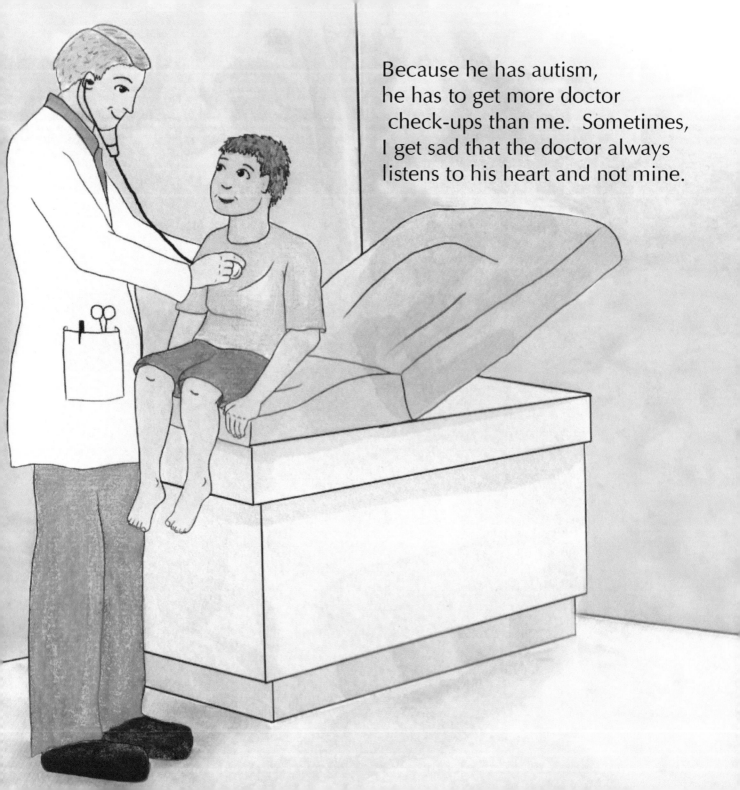

Because he has autism, he has to get more doctor check-ups than me. Sometimes, I get sad that the doctor always listens to his heart and not mine.

I get bored because the appointment is all about him. Last time my mom brought me some books and a game. That helped a lot.

My brother also has a lot of grownup friends that come to the house to play with him. They are called therapists.

It looks like they are playing, but really they
are teaching him important things.
Like how to get along with other kids
and how to use his hands so he can
feed and dress himself.
These things are not easy for him.

Sometimes, they have to work with him alone. This makes me feel left out. I wish people would come over to play with me. I have to find other things to do while they play. I usually draw or build blocks.

Other times, I get to play with them. And I really like the games we play and knowing we are teaching my brother important skills.

Because my brother has autism, some outings are very hard for him. He hears, sees, and smells better than most people, but this can make public places very loud and bright for him. When there is a lot of noise he covers his ears and cries because it hurts.

One time we were all at the fair. My brother got very upset because of all the sounds, smells and lights. We had to leave. This made me very mad because I was having fun. I did not want to leave and I did not understand why he didn't think it was fun.

My mom said my brother couldn't handle such a busy place and that it was painful to him. I did not want him to hurt, but I was still sad we could not enjoy it together.

Even though some outings are too much for my brother, we have found things he really enjoys that we can all do together. He likes museums and aquariums. I think he likes them because they are quiet places, but I like them too. I am happy we have found things we can do as a family.

My mom and dad know that it's important for me to still get to do the things that upset my brother. So sometimes they will take just me on an outing. We go out to dinner and a movie or play at the arcade. This makes me feel very special. I love having mom and dad to myself for a night.

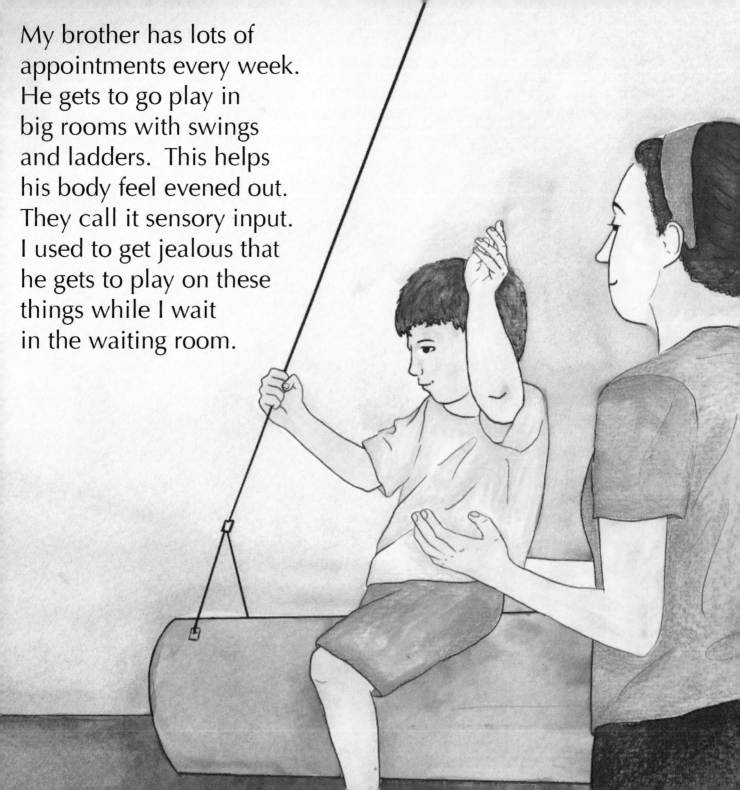

My brother has lots of
appointments every week.
He gets to go play in
big rooms with swings
and ladders. This helps
his body feel evened out.
They call it sensory input.
I used to get jealous that
he gets to play on these
things while I wait
in the waiting room.

Now, I have made friends in the waiting room and I enjoy playing too. I read with my friends or we play with toys. It makes the time go by fast while my brother is getting the sensory input he needs.

I like playing with my brother, but sometimes he has a hard time with his emotions. He is learning how to share and how to play with other kids without getting upset. It makes me sad when he will not share or play with me. Sometimes, I get very mad when he takes something out of my hands or hits me and my mom tells me to walk away.

My brother has rules, but they are different than mine. That's hard for me to understand. My mom explained that my brother does not understand rules the same way and that is what we are trying to teach him. I am learning I need to just follow my rules and let mom worry about my brother's rules. But some days it's still hard.

We are all the happiest when we are playing outside. Even though we like to pretend different things, we can still have fun playing together. My brother is starting to learn how to take turns when we play. His therapists have taught him that everyone is happier when we take turns. I like pretending we are on the Titanic. My brother likes pretending we are digging up dinosaur bones. Both games are super fun.

Sometimes my brother has a very hard time controlling how he acts when he is sad or mad. His therapists call this emotional regulation. It's not his fault that this is hard for him, but it hurts my feelings when he throws things at me or tries to hurt me. I do not like listening to his screaming. It's okay that this upsets me.

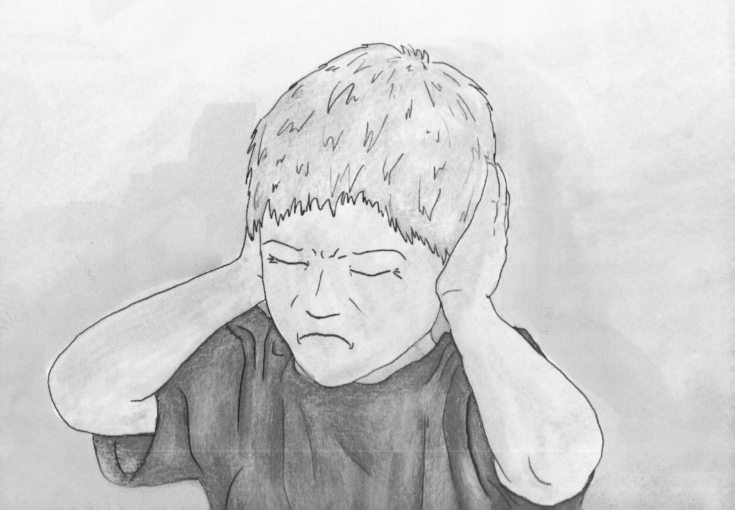

I go to my room while my mom helps
my brother work through whatever is
upsetting him. It makes me sad that my mom
cannot always give me as much attention
as she gives him. Sometimes my mom cries too.
I do not like seeing her cry, but it lets me know
it's okay to cry when it's hard.

At the end of the day we know
we are all in this together and
we will do whatever we
need to do to help my brother
He is a pretty awesome kid
He is my best friend and
I will always look out for him

He has taught me a lot about dinosaurs.
I like watching dinosaur movies with him
because they make him happy.
And that makes me happy.

Being a brother to someone with autism is not always easy.
My mom made me a special room with a lock on the door so that I can have alone time when I need it.

It has helped a lot.

My other favorite thing to do is to play computer games. My brother sometimes watches me play the computer and I know he likes that it makes me happy.

I am a special needs sibling, but I am a lot more than that. Some people say I am typical, but I think I'm anything but typical.

My brother is very special, but I am special too.